Schaum
Christmas Cameos
Level Four

Arranged by Wesley Schaum

Foreword

In response to the enduring popularity of John W. Schaum's *Christmas Cameos* books, these easier versions have been created for a wider range of performers and students.

The thoughtful arrangements in these books are infused with a uniquely fresh appeal. Subtle harmonic nuances accentuate the spiritual quality of the carols and give them a more contemporary feeling. Secular Christmas pieces are arranged in a more casual, sometimes jazzy style.

Distinctive harmonies create unexpected blends of sound, pleasing to the ear. Occasional dissonances enrich the fabric of the music. Accompaniments have a great many imaginative patterns, counter melodies and bass progressions that add interest and appeal.

The music portrays a wide range of emotions subject to individual interpretation. The performer is free to play at different tempos or with rubato, according to personal taste. Likewise, dynamic inflections and pedaling may be added or altered.

The arrangements are suitable for performance in recitals and church programs. If desired, many of the pieces could be combined to make an attractive medley.

The three original Cameo books are at <u>Level 6:</u> *Christmas Cameos* (#11-11), *More Christmas Cameos* (#11-12) and *Still More Christmas Cameos* (#11-13).

Schaum Publications, Inc.
10235 N. Port Washington Rd. • Mequon, WI 53092 • www.schaumpiano.net

Carol of the Bells

M. Leontovich
Words by John W. Schaum

Allegretto ♩ = 126-138
pp Bells car - ol - ing, bells proud - ly ring, They seem to say it's Chist - mas Day.
Bells ev - 'ry - where, fill - ing the air, This is the morn when Christ was born.
p Bells cel - e - brate, bells ded - i - cate, bells praise the Lord with one ac - cord.
mp Let's all re - joice, with hap - py voice, Joy - ful - ly sing hail to the King.
mf Bells har - mo - nize sounds from the skies, Bells clear and bright ring with de - light.

f All hearts are warm when bells per - form music sub - lime at Christ - mas time.
mf Wish - ing you a ver - y Mer - ry Christ - mas, Wish - ing you a ver - y Mer - ry Christ - mas.
mp Bells rang the tone when the Star shone, Bells did pro - claim
when Wise Men came. p Bells ev - 'ry - where fill - ing the air,
This is the morn when Christ was born. meno mosso Bells car - ol - ing! pp

Holly and the Ivy

Andantino ♩ = 100-112
Old French Carol
The hol - ly and the i - vy, When they are both full grown, Of
all the trees that are in the wood, The hol - ly bears the crown. The
ris - ing of the sun, And the run - ning of the deer, The
play - ing of the mer - ry or - gan, Sweet sing - ing in the choir.
mp
mf

God Rest You Merry, Gentlemen

Vivace ♩ = 132-144
Traditional English
mf God rest you mer - ry, gen - tle - men, Let noth - ing you dis - may, Re -
mem - ber Christ our Sav - ior was born on Christ - mas Day, To
f save us all from Sa - tan's pow'r when we were gone a - stray. O
mf ti - dings of com - fort and joy, com - fort and joy, O
ti - dings of com - fort and joy.
rit.
dim.

What Child Is This?

Dolce ♩ = 100-108
Old English Air
What Child is this, Who laid to rest, On
Ma - ry's lap is sleep - - - ing? Whom
an - gels greet with an - thems sweet, While
shep - herds watch are keep - - ing?
cresc.
p
mp

This, this is Christ, the King Whom
shep - herds guard and an - gels sing.
Haste, haste to bring Him laud, the
Babe, the Son of Ma - ry.
mf
mp
rit.
p

Silent Night

Cantabile ♩ = 100-108
Franz Gruber
p Si - lent night! Ho - ly night!
All is calm, all is bright. 'Round yon
vir - gin Moth - er and Child, Ho - ly In - fant so
p
ten - der and mild. Sleep in heav - en - ly peace,
mf
Sleep in heav - en - ly peace.
mp
rit.
p

O Christmas Tree

German Folk Melody

Andante ♩ = 80-88
O Christ - mas Tree! O Christ - mas Tree! Thy leaves are so un -
chang - ing. O Christ - mas Tree! O Christ - mas Tree! Thy
leaves are so un - chang - ing. Not on - ly green when sum - mer's here, But
al - so when 'tis cold and drear. O Christ - mas Tree! O
Christ - mas Tree! Thy leaves are so un - chang - ing.
mf
mp
f

Jingle Bells

Allegro ♩ = 160-176
J. Pierpont
mf
Dash - ing through the snow, In a one - horse o - pen sleigh,
O'er the fields we go, Laugh - ing all the way.
Bells___ on bob - tail ring, Mak - ing spir - its bright. What
fun it is to ride and sing A sleigh - ing song to - night!

f Jin - gle bells! Jin - gle bells! Jin - gle all the way.
Oh, what fun it is to ride In a one - horse o - pen sleigh!
Jin - gle bells! Jin - gle bells! Jin - gle all the way.
Oh, what fun it is to ride In a one - horse o - pen sleigh!
rit.
cresc.
ff

12
Angels We Have Heard On High
Giocoso ♩= 104-116
Traditional French Carol
An - gels we have heard on high, Sweet - ly sing - ing o'er the plains.
And the moun - tains in re - ply, Ech - o - ing their joy - ous strains.
mf Glo - - - - - - - - - - - - - ri - a
in ex - cel - sis De - o, affettuoso f Glo - - - - - -
rit.
- - - - ri - a in ex - cel - sis De - o.

Good King Wenceslas

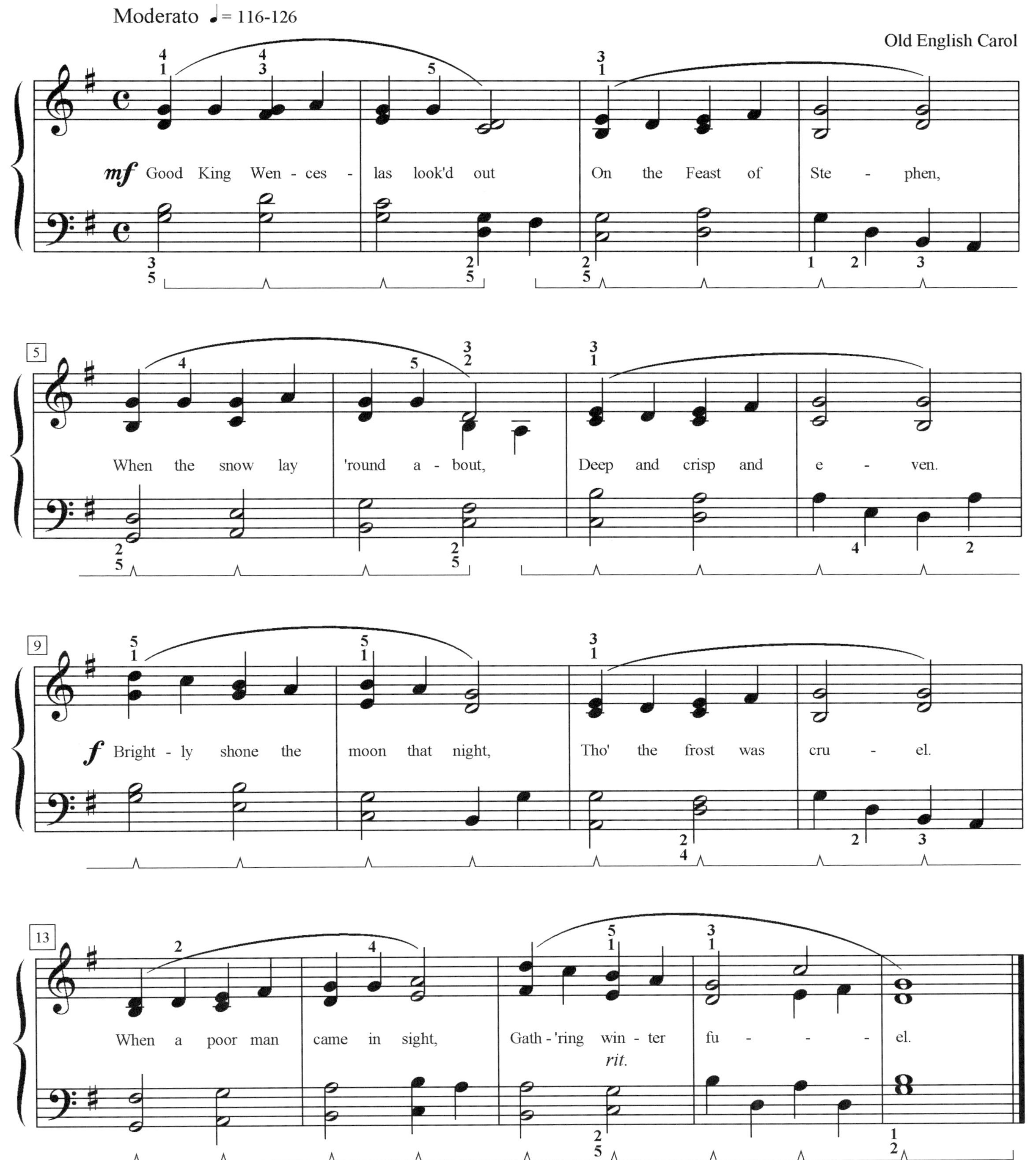

Moderato ♩ = 116-126
Old English Carol
mf Good King Wen - ces - las look'd out On the Feast of Ste - phen,
When the snow lay 'round a - bout, Deep and crisp and e - ven.
f Bright - ly shone the moon that night, Tho' the frost was cru - el.
When a poor man came in sight, Gath - 'ring win - ter fu - el.
rit.

Rise Up, Shepherds and Follow

Andantino ♩ = 100-108 (swing 8ths)
African-American Spiritual
There's a star in the East on Christ-mas morn,___ Rise up, shep-herds and
fol - low.___ It will lead to the place where the Sav - ior's born,___
Rise up, shep-herds and fol - low.___ Leave your sheep and
leave your lambs,___ Rise up, shep - herds and fol - low.___
mf
f

Leave___ your ewes and leave___ your rams,___ Rise up, shep-herds and
fol - low. mp Fol - low, fol - low,
Rise up, shep-herds and fol - low.___ Fol - low the Star of
Beth - le - hem, Rise up, shep-herds and fol - low.___
mf
rit.
f

Hark the Herald Angels Sing

Felix Mendelssohn
Words by Charles Wesley
Maestoso ♩ = 100-108
mf Hark! the her - ald an - gels sing, Glo - ry to the new - born King.
Peace on earth and mer - cy mild, God and sin - ners rec - on - ciled!
Joy - ful, all ye na - tions rise, Join the tri - umph of the skies.
With an - gel - ic hosts pro - claim, Christ is born in Beth - le - hem.
f Hark! the her - ald an - gels sing, Glo - ry to the new - born King.
rit.

Joy To the World

Grandioso ♩= 144-152
George F. Handel
f Joy to the world! The Lord is come. Let
earth re - ceive her King. mf Let
ev - 'ry heart pre - pare Him room, And
heav'n and na - ture sing, And heav'n and na - ture sing, f And
heav'n and heav'n and na - ture sing.

We Wish You a Merry Christmas

Allegro ♩ = 132-144
Old English Carol
mf
We wish you a Mer - ry Christ - mas, We wish you a Mer - ry Christ - mas, We
wish you a Mer - ry Christ - mas and a Hap - py New Year!
mp
Good
tid - ings to you where - ev - er you are.
f
Good
tid - ings for Christ - mas and a Hap - py New Year.
mf

Piu mosso ♩ = 144-152
f

O Come All Ye Faithful

J. F. Wade
Allegretto ♩ = 108-116
mf
O come all ye faith - ful, Joy - ful and tri - um - phant. O
come ye, O come ye to Beth - le - hem.
f Come and be - hold Him, Born the King of an - gels. O
mp
come, let us a - dore Him, O come, let us a - dore Him, O
cresc.
f
come, let us a - dore Him, Christ the Lord.
rit.

Deck the Hall

Theme & Variations

Giocoso ♩ = 132-144
Traditional Welsh
mf
Deck the hall with boughs of hol - ly, Fa la la la la, la la la la.
'Tis the sea - son to be jol - ly, Fa la la la la, la la la la.
mp
Don we now our gay ap - par - el, Fa la la la la la, la la la.
f
Troll the an - cient Yule - tide car - ol, Fa la la la la, la la la la!

Variation I

molto meno mosso
rit.
a tempo
cresc.
molto meno mosso
rit.

Variation II
a tempo
mf
2
1
5
2
basso marcato
5
2
1
mp
2
1
2
5
mf
cresc.
f
rit.
5
4